LONGEVITY COOKBOOK

MEGA BUNDLE – 2 Manuscripts in 1 – 80+ Longevity - friendly recipes including breakfast, side dishes and dessert recipes

TABLE OF CONTENTS

Introduction

Longevity   recipes for personal enjoyment but also for family enjoyment. You will love them for sure for how easy it is to prepare them.

BREAKFAST

BLUEBERRY PANCAKES

Serves: **4**

Prep Time: **10** Minutes

Cook Time: **20** Minutes

Total Time: **30** Minutes

INGREDIENTS

- 1 cup whole wheat flour
- ¼ tsp baking soda
- ¼ tsp baking powder
- 1 cup blueberries
- 2 eggs
- 1 cup milk

DIRECTIONS

1. In a bowl combine all ingredients together and mix well
2. In a skillet heat olive oil
3. Pour ¼ of the batter and cook each pancake for 1-2 minutes per side
4. When ready remove from heat and serve

CHERRY PANCAKES

Serves: *4*
Prep Time: *10* Minutes

Cook Time: *30* Minutes

Total Time: *40* Minutes

INGREDIENTS

- 1 cup whole wheat flour
- ¼ tsp baking soda
- ¼ tsp baking powder
- 1 cup cherries
- 2 eggs
- 1 cup milk

DIRECTIONS

1. In a bowl combine all ingredients together and mix well
2. In a skillet heat olive oil
3. Pour ¼ of the batter and cook each pancake for 1-2 minutes per side
4. When ready remove from heat and serve

BANANA PANCAKES

Serves: **4**

Prep Time: **10**   Minutes

Cook Time: **20**   Minutes

Total Time: **30**   Minutes

INGREDIENTS

- 1 cup whole wheat flour
- ¼ tsp baking soda
- ¼ tsp baking powder
- 1 cup mashed banana
- 2 eggs
- 1 cup milk

DIRECTIONS

1. In a bowl combine all ingredients together and mix well
2. In a skillet heat olive oil
3. Pour ¼ of the batter and cook each pancake for 1-2 minutes per side
4. When ready remove from heat and serve

LIME PANCAKES

Serves: **4**
Prep Time: **10** Minutes
Cook Time: **20** Minutes
Total Time: **30** Minutes

INGREDIENTS

- 1 cup whole wheat flour
- ¼ tsp baking soda
- ¼ tsp baking powder
- 1 cup lime
- 2 eggs
- 1 cup milk

DIRECTIONS

1. In a bowl combine all ingredients together and mix well
2. In a skillet heat olive oil
3. Pour ¼ of the batter and cook each pancake for 1-2 minutes per side
4. When ready remove from heat and serve

GUAVA PANCAKES

Serves: **4**

Prep Time: **10**   Minutes

Cook Time: **30**   Minutes

Total Time: **40**   Minutes

INGREDIENTS

- 1 cup whole wheat flour
- ¼ tsp baking soda
- ¼ tsp baking powder
- 2 eggs
- 1 cup milk
- 1 cup guava

DIRECTIONS

1. In a bowl combine all ingredients together and mix well
2. In a skillet heat olive oil
3. Pour ¼ of the batter and cook each pancake for 1-2 minutes per side
4. When ready remove from heat and serve

APRICOT MUFFINS

Serves: *8-12*
Prep Time: *10*   Minutes

Cook Time: *20*   Minutes

Total Time: *30*   Minutes

INGREDIENTS

- 2 eggs
- 1 tablespoon olive oil
- 1 cup milk
- 2 cups whole wheat flour
- 1 tsp baking soda
- ¼ tsp baking soda
- 1 tsp ginger
- 1 cup apricot
- ¼ cup molasses

DIRECTIONS

1. In a bowl combine all wet ingredients
2. In another bowl combine all dry ingredients
3. Combine wet and dry ingredients together
4. Pour mixture into 8-12 prepared muffin cups, fill 2/3 of the cups
5. Bake for 18-20 minutes at 375 F, when ready remove and serve

PEACH MUFFINS

Serves: **8-12**
Prep Time: **10**   Minutes

Cook Time: **20**   Minutes

Total Time: **30**   Minutes

INGREDIENTS

- 2 eggs
- 1 tablespoon olive oil
- 1 cup milk
- 2 cups whole wheat flour
- 1 tsp baking soda
- ¼ tsp baking soda
- 1 tsp cinnamon
- 1 cup mashed peaches

DIRECTIONS

1. In a bowl combine all wet ingredients
2. In another bowl combine all dry ingredients
3. Combine wet and dry ingredients together
4. Pour mixture into 8-12 prepared muffin cups, fill 2/3 of the cups
5. Bake for 18-20 minutes at 375 F
6. When ready remove from the oven and serve

BLUEBERRY MUFFINS

Serves: *8-12*
Prep Time: *10*   Minutes

Cook Time: *20*   Minutes

Total Time: *30*   Minutes

INGREDIENTS

- 2 eggs
- 1 tablespoon olive oil
- 1 cup milk
- 2 cups whole wheat flour
- 1 tsp baking soda
- ¼ tsp baking soda
- 1 tsp cinnamon
- 1 cup blueberries

DIRECTIONS

1. In a bowl combine all wet ingredients
2. In another bowl combine all dry ingredients
3. Combine wet and dry ingredients together
4. Fold in blueberries and mix well
5. Pour mixture into 8-12 prepared muffin cups, fill 2/3 of the cups
6. Bake for 18-20 minutes at 375 F, when ready remove and serve

PAPAYA MUFFINS

Serves: **8-12**
Prep Time: **10**   Minutes

Cook Time: **20**   Minutes

Total Time: **30**   Minutes

INGREDIENTS

- 2 eggs
- 1 tablespoon olive oil
- 1 cup milk
- 2 cups whole wheat flour
- 1 tsp baking soda
- ¼ tsp baking soda
- 1 tsp cinnamon
- 1 cup papaya

DIRECTIONS

1. In a bowl combine all wet ingredients
2. In another bowl combine all dry ingredients
3. Combine wet and dry ingredients together
4. Pour mixture into 8-12 prepared muffin cups, fill 2/3 of the cups
5. Bake for 18-20 minutes at 375 F
6. When ready remove from the oven and serve

RADISH OMELETTE

Serves: *1*
Prep Time: 5   Minutes

Cook Time: *10*   Minutes

Total Time: *15*   Minutes

INGREDIENTS

- 2 eggs
- ¼ tsp salt
- ¼ tsp black pepper
- 1 tablespoon olive oil
- ¼ cup cheese
- ¼ tsp basil
- 1 cup radish

DIRECTIONS

1. In a bowl combine all ingredients together and mix well
2. In a skillet heat olive oil and pour the egg mixture
3. Cook for 1-2 minutes per side
4. When ready remove omelette from the skillet and serve

ZUCCHINI OMELETTE

Serves: *1*
Prep Time: *5*   Minutes

Cook Time: *10*   Minutes

Total Time: *15*   Minutes

INGREDIENTS

- 2 eggs
- ¼ tsp salt
- ¼ tsp black pepper
- 1 tablespoon olive oil
- ¼ cup cheese
- ¼ tsp basil
- 1 cup zucchini

DIRECTIONS

1. In a bowl combine all ingredients together and mix well
2. In a skillet heat olive oil and pour the egg mixture
3. Cook for 1-2 minutes per side
4. When ready remove omelette from the skillet and serve

CORN OMELETTE

Serves: **1**
Prep Time: **5**   Minutes

Cook Time: **10**   Minutes

Total Time: **15**   Minutes

INGREDIENTS

- 2 eggs
- ¼ tsp salt
- ¼ tsp black pepper
- 1 tablespoon olive oil
- ¼ cup cheese
- ¼ tsp basil
- 1 cup corn

DIRECTIONS

1. In a bowl combine all ingredients together and mix well
2. In a skillet heat olive oil and pour the egg mixture
3. Cook for 1-2 minutes per side
4. When ready remove omelette from the skillet and serve

MUSHROOM OMELETTE

Serves: **1**
Prep Time: **5**   Minutes

Cook Time: **10**   Minutes

Total Time: **15**   Minutes

INGREDIENTS

- 2 eggs
- ¼ tsp salt
- ¼ tsp black pepper
- 1 tablespoon olive oil
- ¼ cup cheese
- ¼ tsp basil
- 1 cup mushrooms

DIRECTIONS

1. In a bowl combine all ingredients together and mix well
2. In a skillet heat olive oil and pour the egg mixture
3. Cook for 1-2 minutes per side
4. When ready remove omelette from the skillet and serve

YAMS OMELETTE

Serves: **1**

Prep Time: **5**   Minutes

Cook Time: **10**   Minutes

Total Time: **15**   Minutes

INGREDIENTS

- 2 eggs
- ¼ tsp salt
- ¼ tsp black pepper
- 1 tablespoon olive oil
- ¼ cup cheese
- ¼ tsp basil
- 1 cup yams

DIRECTIONS

1. In a bowl combine all ingredients together and mix well
2. In a skillet heat olive oil and pour the egg mixture
3. Cook for 1-2 minutes per side
4. When ready remove omelette from the skillet and serve

RAISIN BREAKFAST MIX

Serves: **1**

Prep Time: **5**   Minutes

Cook Time: **5**   Minutes

Total Time: **10**   Minutes

INGREDIENTS

- ½ cup dried raisins
- ½ cup dried pecans
- ¼ cup almonds
- 1 cup coconut milk
- 1 tsp cinnamon

DIRECTIONS

1. In a bowl combine all ingredients together
2. Serve with milk

AVOCADO TOAST

Serves: *2*
Prep Time: *5*   Minutes

Cook Time: *5*   Minutes

Total Time: *10*   Minutes

INGREDIENTS

- 4 slices bread
- 1 avocado
- ¼ tsp red chili flakes
- ¼ tsp salt

DIRECTIONS

1. Toast the bread and set aside
2. Lay avocado slices on each bread slice
3. Sprinkle with red chili flakes and salt
4. Serve when ready

PUMPKIN FRENCH TOAST

Serves: **3**

Prep Time: **5**   Minutes

Cook Time: **15** Minutes

Total Time: **20** Minutes

INGREDIENTS

- ¼ cup milk
- 2 eggs
- ½ cup pumpkin puree
- 1 tablespoon pumpkin slice
- 6 bread slices

DIRECTIONS

1. In a bowl whisk all ingredients for the dipping
2. Dip the bread into the dipping and let it soak for 3-4 minutes
3. In a skillet heat olive oil and fry each slice for 2-3 minutes per side
4. When ready remove from the skillet and serve

COCONUT CHAI OATMEAL

Serves: 2

Prep Time: 5   Minutes

Cook Time: 15   Minutes

Total Time: 20   Minutes

INGREDIENTS

- ¼ cup oats
- ½ cup chia tea
- ¼ cup coconut milk
- 1 peach
- ¼ tsp coconut oil
- 1 tsp coconut flakes

DIRECTIONS

1. In a bowl combine together oats, coconut milk, chia tea and microwave until thickness
2. In a saucepan add peach slices and cook for 2-3 minutes
3. Place peaches over the oats and top with coconut flakes
4. Serve when ready

Serves: **4**

Prep Time: **10** Minutes

Cook Time: **30** Minutes

Total Time: **40** Minutes

INGREDIENTS

- 4 oz. coconut yogurt
- ¼ cup gluten-free granola
- 1 tablespoon cacao nibs
- 1 oz. raspberries

DIRECTIONS

1. Place all ingredients in a bowl and mix well
2. Serve when ready

Serves: *1*
Prep Time: 5   Minutes

Cook Time: 5   Minutes

Total Time: *10*   Minutes

INGREDIENTS

- 2 slices gluten-free toast
- 2 tablespoons peanut butter
- ¼ tsp flax seeds
- ¼ tsp chia seeds

DIRECTIONS

1. Place all ingredients in a bowl and mix well
2. Serve when ready

SAUSAGE BREAKFAST SANDWICH

Serves: **2**
Prep Time: **5**   Minutes

Cook Time: **15**   Minutes

Total Time: **20**   Minutes

INGREDIENTS

- ¼ cup egg substitute
- 1 muffin
- 1 turkey sausage patty
- 1 tablespoon cheddar cheese

DIRECTIONS

1. In a skillet pour egg and cook on low heat
2. Place turkey sausage patty in a pan and cook for 4-5 minutes per side
3. On a toasted muffin place the cooked egg, top with a sausage patty and cheddar cheese
4. Serve when ready

STRAWBERRY MUFFINS

Serves: *8-12*

Prep Time: *10*   Minutes

Cook Time: *20*   Minutes

Total Time: *30*   Minutes

INGREDIENTS

- 2 eggs
- 1 tablespoon olive oil
- 1 cup milk
- 2 cups whole wheat flour
- 1 tsp baking soda
- ¼ tsp baking soda
- 1 tsp cinnamon
- 1 cup strawberries

DIRECTIONS

1. In a bowl combine all dry ingredients
2. In another bowl combine all dry ingredients
3. Combine wet and dry ingredients together
4. Pour mixture into 8-12 prepared muffin cups, fill 2/3 of the cups
5. Bake for 18-20 minutes at 375 F
6. When ready remove from the oven and serve

DESSERTS

BREAKFAST COOKIES

Serves: *8-12*
Prep Time: 5   Minutes

Cook Time: *15*   Minutes

Total Time: *20*   Minutes

INGREDIENTS

- 1 cup rolled oats
- ¼ cup applesauce
- ½ tsp vanilla extract
- 3 tablespoons chocolate chips
- 2 tablespoons dried fruits
- 1 tsp cinnamon

DIRECTIONS

1. Preheat the oven to 325 F
2. In a bowl combine all ingredients together and mix well
3. Scoop cookies using an ice cream scoop
4. Place cookies onto a prepared baking sheet
5. Place in the oven for 12-15 minutes or until the cookies are done
6. When ready remove from the oven and serve

APPLE TART

Serves: **6-8**
Prep Time: **25**   Minutes

Cook Time: **25**   Minutes

Total Time: **50**   Minutes

INGREDIENTS

- pastry sheets

FILLING

- 1 tsp lemon juice
- 3 oz. brown sugar
- 1 lb. apples
- 150 ml double cream
- 2 eggs

DIRECTIONS

1. Preheat oven to 400 F, unfold pastry sheets and place them on a baking sheet
2. Toss together all ingredients together and mix well
3. Spread mixture in a single layer on the pastry sheets
4. Before baking decorate with your desired fruits
5. Bake at 400 F for 22-25 minutes or until golden brown
6. When ready remove from the oven and serve

CHOCHOLATE TART

Serves: *6-8*
Prep Time: 25   Minutes

Cook Time: 25   Minutes

Total Time: *50*   Minutes

INGREDIENTS

- pastry sheets
- 1 tsp vanilla extract
- ½ lb. caramel
- ½ lb. black chocolate
- 4-5 tablespoons butter
- 3 eggs
- ¼ lb. brown sugar

DIRECTIONS

1. Preheat oven to 400 F, unfold pastry sheets and place them on a baking sheet
2. Toss together all ingredients together and mix well
3. Spread mixture in a single layer on the pastry sheets
4. Before baking decorate with your desired fruits
5. Bake at 400 F for 22-25 minutes or until golden brown
6. When ready remove from the oven and serve

OREO PIE

Serves: **8-12**
Prep Time: **15**   Minutes

Cook Time: **35**   Minutes

Total Time: **50**   Minutes

INGREDIENTS

- pastry sheets
- 6-8 oz. chocolate crumb piecrust
- 1 cup half-and-half
- 1 package instant pudding mix
- 10-12 Oreo cookies
- 10 oz. whipped topping

DIRECTIONS

1. Line a pie plate or pie form with pastry and cover the edges of the plate depending on your preference
2. In a bowl combine all pie ingredients together and mix well
3. Pour the mixture over the pastry
4. Bake at 400-425 F for 25-30 minutes or until golden brown
5. When ready remove from the oven and let it rest for 15 minutes

GRAPEFRUIT PIE

Serves: **8-12**
Prep Time: **15**   Minutes

Cook Time: **35**   Minutes

Total Time: **50**   Minutes

INGREDIENTS

- pastry sheets
- 2 cups grapefruit
- 1 cup brown sugar
- ¼ cup flour
- 5-6 egg yolks
- 5 oz. butter

DIRECTIONS

1. Line a pie plate or pie form with pastry and cover the edges of the plate depending on your preference
2. In a bowl combine all pie ingredients together and mix well
3. Pour the mixture over the pastry
4. Bake at 400-425 F for 25-30 minutes or until golden brown
5. When ready remove from the oven and let it rest for 15 minutes

BUTTERFINGER PIE

Serves: **8-12**

Prep Time: **15**   Minutes

Cook Time: **35**   Minutes

Total Time: **50**   Minutes

INGREDIENTS

- pastry sheets
- 1 package cream cheese
- 1 tsp vanilla extract
- ¼ cup peanut butter
- 1 cup powdered sugar (to decorate)
- 2 cups Butterfinger candy bars
- 8 oz whipped topping

DIRECTIONS

1. Line a pie plate or pie form with pastry and cover the edges of the plate depending on your preference
2. In a bowl combine all pie ingredients together and mix well
3. Pour the mixture over the pastry
4. Bake at 400-425 F for 25-30 minutes or until golden brown
5. When ready remove from the oven and let it rest for 15 minutes

SMOOTHIES AND DRINKS

BANANA BREAKFAST SMOOTHIE

Serves: *1*

Prep Time: *5*   Minutes

Cook Time: *5*   Minutes

Total Time: *10*   Minutes

INGREDIENTS

- ½ cup vanilla yogurt
- 2 tsp honey
- Pinch of cinnamon
- 1 banana
- 1 cup ice

DIRECTIONS

1. In a blender place all ingredients and blend until smooth
2. Pour the smoothie in a glass and serve

MACA SMOOTHIE

Serves: *1*

Prep Time: *5*   Minutes

Cook Time: *5*   Minutes

Total Time: *10*   Minutes

INGREDIENTS

- 2 cups hemp milk
- 1 cup ice
- ¼ cup lemon juice
- 2 mangoes
- 1 tablespoon flaxseeds
- 1 tsp maca power
- 1 tsp vanilla extract

DIRECTIONS

1. In a blender place all ingredients and blend until smooth
2. Pour smoothie in a glass and serve

BABY SPINACH SMOOTHIE

Serves: *1*
Prep Time: *5*   Minutes

Cook Time: *5*   Minutes

Total Time: *10*   Minutes

INGREDIENTS

- 1 cup cherry juice
- 1 cup spinach
- 1 cup vanilla yoghurt
- 1 avocado
- 1 cup berries
- 1 tablespoon chia seeds

DIRECTIONS

1. In a blender place all ingredients and blend until smooth
2. Pour smoothie in a glass and serve

SUNRISE SMOOTHIE

Serves: *1*
Prep Time: *5*   Minutes

Cook Time: *5*   Minutes

Total Time: *10*   Minutes

INGREDIENTS

- 1 cup coconut milk
- 1 banana
- ¼ cup lemon juice
- ¼ mango
- 1 tsp almonds
- 1 cup ice

DIRECTIONS

1. In a blender place all ingredients and blend until smooth
2. Pour smoothie in a glass and serve

Serves: **1**

Prep Time: **5**   Minutes

Cook Time: **5**   Minutes

Total Time: **10**   Minutes

INGREDIENTS

- 1 cup vanilla yoghurt
- 1 cup cucumber
- 2 tablespoons dill
- 1 tablespoon basil
- 2 tablespoons mint
- 1 cup ice

DIRECTIONS

1. In a blender place all ingredients and blend until smooth
2. Pour smoothie in a glass and serve

CHERRY SMOOTHIE

Serves: *1*

Prep Time: *5*   Minutes

Cook Time: *5*   Minutes

Total Time: *10*   Minutes

INGREDIENTS

- 1 can cherries
- 2 tablespoons peanut butter
- 1 tablespoon honey
- 1 cup Greek Yoghurt
- 1 cup coconut milk

DIRECTIONS

1. In a blender place all ingredients and blend until smooth
2. Pour smoothie in a glass and serve

CHOCOLATE SMOOTHIE

Serves: *1*
Prep Time: *5*   Minutes

Cook Time: *5*   Minutes

Total Time: *10*   Minutes

INGREDIENTS

- 2 bananas
- 1 cup Greek Yoghurt
- 1 tablespoon honey
- 1 tablespoon cocoa powder
- ½ cup chocolate chips
- ¼ cup almond milk

DIRECTIONS

1. In a blender place all ingredients and blend until smooth
2. Pour smoothie in a glass and serve

TOFU SMOOTHIE

Serves: **1**

Prep Time: **5**   Minutes

Cook Time: **5**   Minutes

Total Time: **10**   Minutes

INGREDIENTS

- 1 cup blueberries
- ¼ cup tofu
- ¼ cup pomegranate juice
- 1 cup ice
- ½ cup agave nectar

DIRECTIONS

1. In a blender place all ingredients and blend until smooth
2. Pour smoothie in a glass and serve

COCONUT SMOOTHIE

Serves: **1**

Prep Time: **5**   Minutes

Cook Time: **5**   Minutes

Total Time: **10**   Minutes

INGREDIENTS

- 1 cup blueberries
- 2 bananas
- 1 cup coconut flakes
- 1 cup coconut milk
- ¼ tsp vanilla essence

DIRECTIONS

1. **In a blender place all ingredients and blend until smooth**
2. **Pour smoothie in a glass and serve**

Serves: *1*
Prep Time: *5*   Minutes

Cook Time: *5*   Minutes

Total Time: *10*   Minutes

INGREDIENTS

- 1 banana
- 1 cup blueberries
- 1 cup vanilla yogurt
- ¼ tablespoon cinnamon
- 1 cup berries

DIRECTIONS

1. **In a blender place all ingredients and blend until smooth**
2. **Pour smoothie in a glass and serve**

KIWI SMOOTHIE

Serves: *1*
Prep Time: *5*   Minutes

Cook Time: *5*   Minutes

Total Time: *10*   Minutes

INGREDIENTS

- 2 mangoes
- 1 tablespoon honey
- 1 cup yogurt
- 2 kiwis
- 1 cup ice
- 1 cup spinach
- ¼ tsp mint

DIRECTIONS

1. In a blender place all ingredients and blend until smooth
2. Pour smoothie in a glass and serve

SECOND COOKBOOK

ZUCCHINI SOUP

Serves: **4**

Prep Time: **10**   Minutes

Cook Time: **20**   Minutes

Total Time: **30**   Minutes

INGREDIENTS

- 1 tablespoon olive oil
- 1 lb. zucchini
- ¼ red onion
- ½ cup all-purpose flour
- ¼ tsp salt
- ¼ tsp pepper
- 1 can vegetable broth
- 1 cup heavy cream

DIRECTIONS

1. In a saucepan heat olive oil and sauté zucchini until tender
2. Add remaining ingredients to the saucepan and bring to a boil

3. When all the vegetables are tender transfer to a blender and blend until smooth

4. Pour soup into bowls, garnish with parsley and serve

CUCUMBER SOUP

Serves: **2**

Prep Time: **10** Minutes

Cook Time: **20** Minutes

Total Time: **30** Minutes

INGREDIENTS

- 2 tablespoons olive oil
- 2 cloves garlic
- ¼ cup lemon juice
- ¼ cup parsley
- ¼. cup cilantro
- ¼ cup greens
- 1 cup baby spinach
- 2 cups cucumber
- Salt
- radishes

DIRECTIONS

1. In a blender add all ingredients and blend until smooth
2. Season and refrigerate the soup
3. When ready pour soup into bowl and serve

VEGETARIAN MINESTRONE SOUP

Serves: *5*

Prep Time: *10*   Minutes

Cook Time: *40*   Minutes

Total Time: *50*   Minutes

INGREDIENTS

- 1 tablespoon olive oil
- ¾ cup onion
- 2 ½ cups water
- 2 cups zucchini
- 1 cup sliced carrots
- 1 cup beans
- ¼ cup celery
- 2 tablespoons basil
- 1/3 tsp oregano
- ¼ tsp black pepper
- 1 can plum tomatoes
- 2 cloves garlic
- ½ cup uncooked pasta

DIRECTIONS

1. In a saucepan add oil, onion and sauté for 4-5 minutes

2. Add remaining ingredients and bring to a boil

3. Reduce heat and simmer on low heat for 20-25 minutes

4. Add pasta and cook until pasta is al dente for 10-12 minutes

5. When ready, remove from heat and serve

CABBAGE STEW

Serves: *4*

Prep Time: *10*   Minutes

Cook Time: *40*   Minutes

Total Time: *50*   Minutes

INGREDIENTS

- 1 lb. bison
- 1 tablespoon olive oil
- ¼ cabbage
- 2 carrots
- 1 onion
- 2 cloves garlic
- 2 tablespoons aminos
- 4 cups chicken stock

DIRECTIONS

1. In a pot sauté the carrot, onion and cabbage for 2-3 minutes
2. Add bison and cook for 4-5 minutes
3. Add chicken stock, garlic, ginger and coconut aminos
4. Cook for 25-30 minutes
5. When ready from heat garnish with pepper and serve

CHICKEN RICE SOUP

Serves: **4**

Prep Time: **10** Minutes

Cook Time: **40** Minutes

Total Time: **50** Minutes

INGREDIENTS

- 1 tablespoon olive oil
- 1 cup carrot
- 1 cup onion
- 1 cup celery
- 1 chicken breast
- 2 cloves garlic
- 6 cups chicken broth
- ½ cup brown rice
- ¼ cup lemon juice
- 1 tsp black pepper
- ¼ cup parsley

DIRECTIONS

1. In a pot sauté the carrot, onion and celery for 2-3 minutes
2. Add chicken breast and cook for another 4-5 minutes
3. Add rice, lemon juice, pepper and chicken broth

4. Cook for 30-40 minutes on high heat
5. When soup is cooked remove from heat
6. Garnish with parsley and serve

MISO SOUP

Serves: **2**

Prep Time: **10** Minutes

Cook Time: **20** Minutes

Total Time: **30** Minutes

INGREDIENTS

- 2 tablespoons arame
- 1 cup water
- 2 cups chicken broth
- 1 cup mushrooms
- 2 tablespoons miso paste
- 10 oz. codfish fillet
- 2 cups vegetables
- ¼ cup broccoli sprouts
- 1 tablespoon scallion
- 1 tablespoon olive oil

DIRECTIONS

1. In a bowl soak arame and set aside
2. In a saucepan add broth and bring to a boil
3. Add the cod to the saucepan, vegetables. cover and cook for 5-6 minutes
4. Stir in the miso paste and cook until soup is ready

5. Ladle into bowls top with scallions and serve

MUSHROOM SOUP

Serves: *6*
Prep Time: *20*   Minutes

Cook Time: *35*   Minutes

Total Time: *55*   Minutes

INGREDIENTS

- 2 tablespoons olive oil
- 2 onions
- 2 celery sticks
- 4 garlic cloves
- 4 sprigs of rosemary
- 3 carrots
- 3 cups mushrooms
- 4 cups vegetable broth
- 2 bay leaves

DIRECTIONS

1. In a saucepan sauté garlic, celery, onions until soft
2. Add mushrooms, carrots and sauté for another 4-5 minutes
3. Add bay leaves, broth and simmer for 25-30 minutes
4. When ready remove from heat and serve

CHICKEN SOUP

Serves: *4*

Prep Time: *15* Minutes

Cook Time: *50* Minutes

Total Time: *65* Minutes

INGREDIENTS

- 1 chicken
- 2 tablespoons coconut oil
- 2 l water
- 2 tablespoons apple cider vinegar
- 2 onions
- 6 carrots
- 5 celery sticks
- 2 zucchinis
- 1-inch ginger root
- 4 cloves garlic
- 1 bunch parsley

DIRECTIONS

1. Cut chicken into pieces and place in a pot
2. Add water, vinegar, parsley and boil for 50-60 minutes
3. Meanwhile add the rest of the ingredients

4. Simmer for 5-6 hours on low heat
5. When ready remove from heat and serve

ASPARAGUS SOUP

Serves: **4**

Prep Time: **10**   Minutes

Cook Time: **50**   Minutes

Total Time: **60**   Minutes

INGREDIENTS

- 8 oz. fennel bulbs
- 10 oz. asparagus
- 1 bunch onions
- 3 cups water
- 1 tsp salt
- 2 tablespoons rice
- 2 leeks
- 2 tablespoons sesame oil
- ¼ cup dill
- ¼ cup mint leaves
- 2 cups vegetable broth
- 2 tablespoons lemon juice

DIRECTIONS

1. In a skillet heat olive oil and sauté onion, dill and mint leaves
2. Slice the vegetables and place them in a pot

3. Add salt, rice, water and simmer for 35-45 minutes

4. Add sautéed ingredients to the soup and simmer for another 4-5 minutes

5. When ready blend the soup and serve

SEASWEED SOUP

Serves: 2
Prep Time: 15   Minutes

Cook Time: 20   Minutes

Total Time: 35   Minutes

INGREDIENTS

- 2 cups water
- 1 tablespoon soy sauce
- 2 oz. seaweed
- ¼ cup tofu
- 1-inch ginger
- 1 tsp olive oil
- 2 garlic cloves
- 4 scallions

DIRECTIONS

1. In a soup pot add water, scallion, ginger, garlic and bring to a boil
2. In a skillet heat olive oil and sauté tofu
3. Add sautéed tofu to the soup and the rest of the ingredients
4. Cook until soup is cooked
5. When ready remove from heat garnish with scallions and serve

SIDE DISHES

SESAME PORK TACOS

Serves: **4**

Prep Time: **5** Minutes

Cook Time: **15** Minutes

Total Time: **25** Minutes

INGREDIENTS

- 1 cup cucumber slices
- 5 radishes
- ½ cup red wine vinegar
- 3 tsp sugar
- 1 tablespoon olive oil
- 3 scallions
- 1 cup red cabbage
- 1 lb. ground pork
- 2 tsp garlic powder
- 2 tablespoons sesame oil
- 2 tablespoons soy sauce
- 1 tsp Sriracha
- 10 tortillas
- 1 tsp cilantro
- ¼ cup sour cream

DIRECTIONS

1. In a bowl add radishes, cucumbers, vinegar, 1 tsp sugar and salt, stir well to combine
2. In a pan add oil, scallions, cabbage and cook for 4-5 minutes
3. Add pork, sugar, garlic powder and cook for another 4-5 minutes
4. Add soy sauce, sesame oil and stir to combine
5. Spread sour cream in the center of your tortilla, add pork filling and sprinkle cilantro, radishes and top with meat mixture

WATERMELON GAZPACHO

Serves: *3*
Prep Time: *10* Minutes

Cook Time: *10* Minutes

Total Time: *20* Minutes

INGREDIENTS

- 2 cups ripe watermelon
- 1 red pepper
- ¼ onion
- 3 tablespoons red wine vinegar
- 6 tablespoons cranberry juice
- Italian basil leaves as needed

DIRECTIONS

1. Puree all ingredients, except the basil, until smooth
2. Refrigerate to chill
3. Serve garnished with basil, onion, tomato or cucumber

LIME GRILLED CORN

Serves: **3**
Prep Time: **5**   Minutes

Cook Time: **15**   Minutes

Total Time: **20**   Minutes

INGREDIENTS

- 3 ears of corn
- 2 tablespoons mayonnaise
- 2 tablespoons squeezed lime juice
- ½ tsp chili powder
- 1 pinch of salt

DIRECTIONS

1. Place corn onto the grill and cook for 5-6 minutes or until the kernels being to brown
2. Turn every few minutes until all sides are slightly charred
3. In a bowl mix the rest of ingredients
4. Spread a light coating of the mixture onto each cob and serve

MACADAMIA DIP WITH VEGETABLES

Serves: **4**

Prep Time: **10**   Minutes

Cook Time: **30**   Minutes

Total Time: **40**   Minutes

INGREDIENTS

- 6 oz. squash
- ½ bunch basil
- ¼ cup macadamia nuts
- 1 tablespoon olive oil
- ¼ lemon
- ¼ tsp ground smoked paprika
- salt
- vegetable sticks

DIRECTIONS

1. Preheat the oven to 350 F
2. Cut the squash into chunks and roast for 25-30 minutes
3. In a food processor add the basil leaves, lemon zest, macadamia nuts, squash pieces and salt
4. Serve with vegetable sticks: cucumber, carrots, tomatoes and green pepper

GINGERSNAPS

Serves: *6*
Prep Time: *10* Minutes

Cook Time: *15* Minutes

Total Time: *25* Minutes

INGREDIENTS

- 1 cup white whole wheat flour
- 1 cornstarch
- 1 tsp baking powder
- 1 tsp ground ginger
- ½ tsp ground cinnamon
- ¼ tsp nutmeg
- ¼ tsp ground cloves
- 1 tablespoon unsalted butter
- 1 egg white
- 2 tsp vanilla stevia
- ½ cup nonfat milk
- ½ cup molasses
- 1 tsp vanilla extract

DIRECTIONS

1. Preheat the oven to 350 F

2. In a bowl whisk together the cornstarch, ginger, baking powder, cinnamon, nutmeg, cloves and salt and flour

3. In another bowl mix vanilla extract, egg, butter, stevia, molasses and milk

4. Add in the flour mixture and stir until fully incorporated

5. Divide dough into 14-16 portions and roll each into a ball

6. Place onto a baking sheet and press it down into the cookie dough

7. Bake for 8-10 minutes

8. When ready, remove and serve

TURKEY & VEGGIES STUFFED PEPPERS

Serves: **4**

Prep Time: **10**   Minutes

Cook Time: **40**   Minutes

Total Time: **50**   Minutes

INGREDIENTS

- 4 red bell peppers
- 1 lb. ground turkey
- 1 tablespoon olive oil
- ¼ onion
- 1 cup mushrooms 1 zucchini
- ½ green bell pepper
- ½ yellow bell pepper
- 1 cup spinach
- 1 can diced tomatoes
- 1 tsp Italian seasoning
- ¼ tsp garlic powder
- 1 pinch of salt

DIRECTIONS

1. Preheat the oven to 325 F
2. In a pot bring water to boil, add pepper and cook for 5-6 minutes

3. In a skillet cook the turkey until brown and set aside

4. In another pan add onion, olive oil, mushrooms, zucchini, green, yellow pepper, spinach and cook until tender

5. Add remaining ingredients to the turkey and cook until done

6. Stuff the peppers with the mixture and place them into a casserole dish

7. Bake for 15-18 minutes or until done

QUINOA TACO MEAT

Serves: **6**
Prep Time: **10** Minutes

Cook Time: **50** Minutes

Total Time: **60** Minutes

INGREDIENTS

- 1 cup red quinoa
- 1 cup vegetable broth
- ¾ cup water

SEASONING

- ¼ cup salsa
- 1 tablespoon yeast
- 1 tsp cumin
- 1 tsp chili powder
- ¼ tsp garlic powder
- ½ tsp black pepper
- ½ tsp salt
- 1 tablespoon olive oil

DIRECTIONS

1. In a saucepan add quinoa and cook for 5-6 minutes
2. Add water, vegetable broth and bring to a boil

3. Reduce heat to low and cook for 20-22 minutes or until liquid is absorbed

4. Add quinoa to a mixing bowl, remaining ingredients and toss to combine

5. Bake for 25-30 minutes or until golden brown

6. When ready remove and serve with taco salads, enchiladas or nachos

KALE CHIPS

Serves: **6**

Prep Time: **10**   Minutes

Cook Time: **25**   Minutes

Total Time: **35**   Minutes

INGREDIENTS

- 1 bunch of kale
- 1 tablespoon olive oil
- 1 tsp salt

DIRECTIONS

1. Preheat the oven to 325 F
2. Chop the kale into chip size pieces
3. Put pieces into a bowl tops with olive oil and salt
4. Spread the leaves in a single layer onto a parchment paper
5. Bake for 20-25 minutes
6. When ready, remove and serve

CHICKEN AND BROWN RICE PASTA

Serves: **2**
Prep Time: **10**   Minutes

Cook Time: **15**   Minutes

Total Time: **25**   Minutes

INGREDIENTS

- 1 cup cooked rice pasta
- 1 chicken breast
- ¼ cup no sugar marinara sauce
- ½ cup tomatoes
- parsley for serving
- 1 tsp olive oil

DIRECTIONS

1. In a skillet cook the pasta according to the package directions
2. Drain and rinse the pasta
3. Add cooked chicken breast, marinara sauce and serve

PHILLY CHEESE STEAK

Serves: **4**

Prep Time: **5**   Minutes

Cook Time: **20**   Minutes

Total Time: **25**   Minutes

INGREDIENTS

- 2 tsp olive oil
- 1 onion
- 3 portobello mushrooms
- 1 red bell pepper
- 1 tsp dried oregano
- ¼ tsp ground pepper
- 1 tablespoon all-purpose flour
- ½ cup vegetable broth
- 1 tablespoon soy sauce
- 2 oz. vegan cheese
- 3 whole-wheat rolls

DIRECTIONS

1. In a skillet add onion, pepper, bell pepper, oregano and cook until soft
2. Reduce heat, sprinkle flour, soy sauce, broth and bring to a simmer

3. Remove from heat, add cheese slices on top and let it stand until fully melted
4. Divide into 3-4 portions and serve

CAULIFLOWER WINGS

Serves: **4**

Prep Time: **10**   Minutes

Cook Time: **50**   Minutes

Total Time: **60**   Minutes

INGREDIENTS

- 1 head cauliflower
- ¼ unsweetened almond milk
- ¼ cup water
- ¾ rice flour
- 1 tsp garlic powder
- 1 tsp onion powder
- 1 tsp cumin
- 1 tsp paprika
- ½ tsp salt
- ¼ tsp ground pepper
- bbq sauce

VINEGAR SAUCE
- 1 tablespoon vegan butter
- 2 tablespoons apple cider vinegar
- 1 tablespoon water
- 1 pinch of salt

DIRECTIONS

1. Preheat the oven to 425 F
2. Mix all wing ingredients in a bowl and submerge each cauliflower floret into the mix
3. Place florets on a prepare baking sheet
4. Bake for 10 minutes, flip and bake for another 10 minutes or until golden brown
5. Remove the cauliflower from the oven and serve with vinegar sauce
6. When ready season with pepper and salt and serve

ROASTED BOK CHOY

Serves: **4**

Prep Time: **5**   Minutes

Cook Time: **15**   Minutes

Total Time: **20**   Minutes

INGREDIENTS

- 5 heads baby bok choy
- olive oil
- 1 tsp pepper
- 1 tsp salt

DIRECTIONS

1. Preheat the oven to 425 F
2. Cut each bok choy in half lengthwise and place on a baking sheet
3. Drizzle with olive oil, pepper and salt
4. Bake for 10-12 minutes, flip and bake for another 8-10 minutes
5. When ready remove and serve

GREEN PESTO PASTA

Serves: 2

Prep Time: 5   Minutes

Cook Time: 15   Minutes

Total Time: 20   Minutes

INGREDIENTS

- 4 oz. spaghetti
- 2 cups basil leaves
- 2 garlic cloves
- ¼ cup olive oil
- 2 tablespoons parmesan cheese
- ½ tsp black pepper

DIRECTIONS

7. Bring water to a boil and add pasta
8. In a blend add parmesan cheese, basil leaves, garlic and blend
9. Add olive oil, pepper and blend again
10. Pour pesto onto pasta and serve when ready

TACO SALAD

Serves: **2**
Prep Time: **5**   Minutes

Cook Time: **5**   Minutes

Total Time: **10**   Minutes

INGREDIENTS

- ½ cup olive oil
- 1 lb. cooked steak
- 1 tablespoon taco seasoning
- Juice of 1 lime
- 1 tsp cumin
- 1 head romaine lettuce
- 1 cup corn
- 1 cup beans
- 1 cup tomatoes

DIRECTIONS

1. In a bowl mix all ingredients and mix well
2. Serve with dressing

KALE SALAD

Serves: **2**

Prep Time: **5**   Minutes

Cook Time: **5**   Minutes

Total Time: **10**   Minutes

INGREDIENTS

- 2 cups kale
- 1 tablespoon hemp seeds
- 1 cucumber
- 1 tsp honey
- 1 tsp olive oil
- 1 handful parsley

DIRECTIONS

1. **In a bowl mix all ingredients and mix well**
2. **Serve with dressing**

Serves: **2**

Prep Time: **5**   Minutes

Cook Time: **5**   Minutes

Total Time: **10** Minutes

INGREDIENTS

- 1 cup cauliflower
- 1 cup broccoli
- 1 cup brussels sprouts
- 1 cup red bell pepper
- 1 cup squash
- 1 tablespoon olive oil

DIRECTIONS

1. In a bowl mix all ingredients and mix well
2. Serve with dressing

Serves: **2**

Prep Time: **5**   Minutes

Cook Time: **5**   Minutes

Total Time: **10** Minutes

INGREDIENTS

- ½ cauliflower florets
- 1 cup pumpkin
- 1 cup Brussel sprouts
- 1 cup quinoa
- 1 tablespoon olive oil

DIRECTIONS

1. In a bowl mix all ingredients and mix well
2. Serve with dressing

Serves: **2**
Prep Time: **5**   Minutes

Cook Time: **5**   Minutes

Total Time: **10**   Minutes

INGREDIENTS

- 2 red chicory
- 2 fennel bulbs
- ½ cup watercress
- 2 garlic cloves
- 1 tablespoon olive oil

DIRECTIONS

1. In a bowl mix all ingredients and mix well
2. Serve with dressing

Serves: **2**

Prep Time: **5**   Minutes

Cook Time: **5**   Minutes

Total Time: **10**   Minutes

INGREDIENTS

- 1 fennel bulb
- 1 tablespoon lemon juice
- ¼ cup olive oil
- 1 tsp mint
- 1 tsp onion

DIRECTIONS

1. In a bowl mix all ingredients and mix well
2. Serve with dressing

Serves: 2
Prep Time: 5   Minutes

Cook Time: 5   Minutes

Total Time: *10*   Minutes

INGREDIENTS

- 2 lb. sweet potatoes
- ¼ cup olive oil
- 2 tablespoons lemon juice
- ¼ cup scallions
- ¼ cup cilantro
- ¼ tsp salt

DIRECTIONS

1. In a bowl mix all ingredients and mix well
2. Serve with dressing

WATERCRESS FRITATTA

Serves: **2**
Prep Time: **10** Minutes

Cook Time: **20** Minutes

Total Time: **30** Minutes

INGREDIENTS

- ½ lb. watercress
- 1 tablespoon olive oil
- ½ red onion
- ¼ tsp salt
- 2 oz. cheddar cheese
- 1 garlic clove
- ¼ tsp dill

DIRECTIONS

1. In a bowl whisk eggs with salt and cheese
2. In a frying pan heat olive oil and pour egg mixture
3. Add remaining ingredients and mix well
4. Serve when ready

KALE FRITATTA

Serves: *2*

Prep Time: *10* Minutes

Cook Time: *20* Minutes

Total Time: *30* Minutes

INGREDIENTS

- 1 cup kale
- 1 tablespoon olive oil
- ½ red onion
- ¼ tsp salt
- 2 oz. cheddar cheese
- 1 garlic clove
- ¼ tsp dill

DIRECTIONS

1. In a skillet sauté kale until tender
2. In a bowl whisk eggs with salt and cheese
3. In a frying pan heat olive oil and pour egg mixture
4. Add remaining ingredients and mix well
5. When ready serve with sautéed kale

MEDITERRANENA BUDDA BOWL

Serves: **1**
Prep Time: **10** Minutes

Cook Time: **10** Minutes

Total Time: **20** Minutes

INGREDIENTS

- 1 zucchini
- ¼ tsp oregano
- Salt
- 1 cup cooked quinoa
- 1 cup spinach
- 1 cup mixed greens
- ½ cup red pepper
- ¼ cup cucumber
- ¼ cup tomatoes
- parsley
- tahini dressing

DIRECTIONS

1. **In a skillet heat olive oil olive and sauté zucchini until soft and sprinkle oregano over zucchini**

2. In a bowl add the rest of ingredients and toss to combine
3. Add fried zucchini and mix well
4. Pour over tahini dressing, mix well and serve

VEGAN CURRY

Serves: **4**
Prep Time: **10** Minutes

Cook Time: **20** Minutes

Total Time: **30** Minutes

INGREDIENTS

- 1 tablespoon olive oil
- ¼ cup onion
- 2 stalks celery
- 1 garlic clove
- ¼ tsp coriander
- ¼ tsp cumin
- ¼ tsp turmeric
- ¼ tsp red pepper flakes
- 1 cauliflower
- 1 zucchini
- 2 tomatoes
- 1 tsp salt
- 1 cup vegetable broth
- 1 handful of baby spinach
- 1 tablespoon almonds
- 1 tablespoon cilantro

DIRECTIONS

1. In a skillet heat olive oil and sauté celery, garlic and onions for 4-5 minutes or until vegetables are tender

2. Add cumin, spices, coriander, cumin, turmeric red pepper flakes stir to combine and cook for another 1-2 minutes

3. Add zucchini, cauliflower, tomatoes, broth, spinach, water and simmer on low heat for 15-20 minutes

4. Add remaining ingredients and simmer for another 4-5 minutes

5. Garnish curry and serve

CAULIFLOWER WITH ROSEMARY

Serves: **2**

Prep Time: **5** Minutes

Cook Time: **15** Minutes

Total Time: **20** Minutes

INGREDIENTS

- 1 cauliflower
- 1 tablespoon rosemary
- 1 cup vegetable stock
- 2 garlic cloves
- salt

DIRECTIONS

1. In a saucepan add cauliflower, stock and bring to a boil for 12-15 minutes
2. Blend cauliflower until smooth, add garlic, salt, rosemary and blend again
3. When ready pour in a bowl and serve

BRUSSELS SPROUTS

Serves: *2*
Prep Time: *10*   Minutes

Cook Time: *20*   Minutes

Total Time: *30*   Minutes

INGREDIENTS

- 1 tablespoon olive oil
- 2 shallots
- 2 cloves garlic
- 1 lb. brussels sprouts
- 1 cup vegetable stock
- 4 springs thyme
- ¼ cup pine nuts

DIRECTIONS

1. In a pan heat olive oil and cook shallots until tender
2. Add garlic, sprouts, thyme, stock and cook for another 4-5 minutes
3. Cover and cook for another 10-12 minutes or until sprouts are soft
4. When ready add pine nuts and serve

PIZZA

SIMPLE PIZZA RECIPE

Serves: **6-8**

Prep Time: **10**   Minutes

Cook Time: **15**   Minutes

Total Time: **25**   Minutes

INGREDIENTS

- 1 pizza crust
- ½ cup tomato sauce
- ¼ black pepper
- 1 cup pepperoni slices
- 1 cup mozzarella cheese
- 1 cup olives

DIRECTIONS

1. Spread tomato sauce on the pizza crust
2. Place all the toppings on the pizza crust
3. Bake the pizza at 425 F for 12-15 minutes
4. When ready remove pizza from the oven and serve

Serves: *6-8*
Prep Time: *10*   Minutes
Cook Time: *15*   Minutes
Total Time: *25*   Minutes

INGREDIENTS

- 1 pizza crust
- ½ cup tomato sauce
- ¼ black pepper
- 1 cup zucchini slices
- 1 cup mozzarella cheese
- 1 cup olives

DIRECTIONS

1. Spread tomato sauce on the pizza crust
2. Place all the toppings on the pizza crust
3. Bake the pizza at 425 F for 12-15 minutes
4. When ready remove pizza from the oven and serve

Serves: **6-8**
Prep Time: **10**   Minutes

Cook Time: **15**   Minutes

Total Time: **25**   Minutes

INGREDIENTS

- 1 pizza crust
- ½ cup tomato sauce
- ¼ black pepper
- 1 cup cauliflower
- 1 cup mozzarella cheese
- 1 cup olives

DIRECTIONS

1. Spread tomato sauce on the pizza crust
2. Place all the toppings on the pizza crust
3. Bake the pizza at 425 F for 12-15 minutes
4. When ready remove pizza from the oven and serve

BROCCOLI RECIPE

Serves: *6-8*
Prep Time: *10*   Minutes

Cook Time: *15*   Minutes

Total Time: *25*   Minutes

INGREDIENTS

- 1 pizza crust
- ½ cup tomato sauce
- ¼ black pepper
- 1 cup broccoli
- 1 cup mozzarella cheese
- 1 cup olives

DIRECTIONS

1. Spread tomato sauce on the pizza crust
2. Place all the toppings on the pizza crust
3. Bake the pizza at 425 F for 12-15 minutes
4. When ready remove pizza from the oven and serve

Serves: **6-8**
Prep Time: **10**   Minutes

Cook Time: **15**   Minutes

Total Time: **25**   Minutes

INGREDIENTS

- 1 pizza crust
- ½ cup tomato sauce
- ¼ black pepper
- 1 cup pepperoni slices
- 1 cup tomatoes
- 6-8 ham slices
- 1 cup mozzarella cheese
- 1 cup olives

DIRECTIONS

1. Spread tomato sauce on the pizza crust
2. Place all the toppings on the pizza crust
3. Bake the pizza at 425 F for 12-15 minutes
4. When ready remove pizza from the oven and serve

THANK YOU FOR READING THIS BOOK!

CPSIA information can be obtained
at www.ICGtesting.com
Printed in the USA
BVHW032147120321
602396BV00022B/147